Then & Now
RHONDDA
FROM CWMPARC TO BLAENCWM

Carmel Chapel Sunday School, 1993. The chapel was opened on 20 March 1859 in Baglan Street, Penyreglyn. Prior to the building of the chapel on Baglan Street, the members met for a short while in a meeting room over the stables of the Bute Hotel in Bute Street, Treherbert. Sadly, the Sunday School closed during 1998 due to lack of attendance. Left to right, back row: Gareth Morgan-Jones, Vivienne Evans, Matthew Evans, -?-, Dewi Todd Jones, -?-, Iris Griffiths (concert director). Front row: -?-, -?-, Thomas ?, Hannah Francis, Geraint Francis, -?-, -?-, -?-.

Front cover illustration: Residents of Scott Street Tynewydd gather to celebrate the coronation of Queen Elizabeth II.

Then & Now
RHONDDA
FROM CWMPARC TO BLAENCWM

*This book is dedicated to the memories of my father Ivor Williams
and fellow historian John Henry Landon Thomas, 'Jack',
both of whom encouraged my interest in local history.*

COMPILED BY SEAN JAMES CAMERON

TEMPUS

First published 2001
Copyright © Sean James Cameron, 2001

Tempus Publishing Limited
The Mill, Brimscombe Port,
Stroud, Gloucestershire, GL5 2QG

ISBN 0 7524 2060 7

Typesetting and origination by
Tempus Publishing Limited
Printed in Great Britain by
Midway Clark Printing, Wiltshire

FOREWORD

Rhondda 1879: We learn from reports on this period that religion had reached a very low ebb in the Rhondda. Entertainment had become the vogue. Amusements such as dancing, travelling fairs and theatres were all the craze. The rapid growth of population brought many changes, many of which undermined the former ordered life of the community. Small taverns became large public houses and were made more comfortable with a private room for the selected customers who did not wish it to be known that they were indulging in alcoholic drinks. The drinking influence cast a shadow over the miners' home life. Fighting became a common sight, gambling groups played cards on the mountain side, bare fist fighting, dog fights, and an increase in lawlessness demanded an influx of law and order and an increase in the numbers of police. The groups of young people who used to frequent street corners for conversation and impromptu singing were soon 'moved on' by the constabulary, moving them into public houses and increasing the problem of young drinkers.

The exact time of the religious revival in the Rhondda is difficult to find; one of the main events which contributed to the increased religious activity must be the meeting on the Bute Square in 1879. A crowd had gathered on the square, how many out of curiosity we shall never know, before a man and woman, well dressed and smiling, appeared. The man carried a concertina which he began to play, the tune was lively and catchy, and the woman, a soprano, began to sing. She sang a simple gospel hymn and soon the crowd began singing. This was the first appearance of Captain and Mrs Hayter, and along with Pentre residents, Ms Kate Shepherd and her mother, the first Salvation Army in the Rhondda was established.

Soon the public houses lost their customers to religion. Ministers and vicars became less prejudiced and the teachings and influences of the churches and chapels gave a new outlook on life and change was to be seen in peoples' homes and work places.

The late Ivor Williams

Contents

Foreword 4

Acknowledgements 6

Introduction 7

1. Blaencwm (Head of the Valley) 9
2. Blaenrhondda (Head of the Rhondda) 19
3. Tynewydd (New House) 25
4. Treherbert (The Three Herberts) 39
5. Penyrenglyn (Home of the Angel) 59
6. Treorchy (Home of the River Orkwy) 69
7. Cwmparc (Valley of Parkland) 89
8. Through the Years 95

The Author

Sean James Cameron was born at Llwynypia Hospital on 23 April 1974 in the Rhondda Valleys and was brought up in Penyrenglyn at the head of the Rhondda Fawr, first living on Hopkin Street before moving to Eleanor Street at the age of one. He attended Penyrenglyn Infants and Juniors School before moving onto Pentre Grammar School and subsequently Treorchy Comprehensive School.

By the age of sixteen Sean had become a well-known figure in the Treherbert community through his activities with the Selsig Amateur Operatic Society under the direction of Gwenno Cole-Evans. He was also involved in Treherbert and District Gardening Society and Carmel Chapel as well as being one of the founder members of the Treherbert and District Forum. He worked as Regional Correspondent for the *Rhondda Leader* newspaper and *South Wales Echo*.

In 1996 he moved to Cardiff to pursue a career in television and film. Living on Colum Road Cathays for a year, he later moved to Canton, where he currently resides and works as a television/film producer and editor.

Acknowledgments

I would like to take this opportunity to thank the following people for the loan of their photographs: Ivor Williams Collection, Elizabeth Harris 'Betty' (Tynewydd), John Henry Landon Thomas Collection, Treorchy Library, Alan Gunton (pp. 22 and 66), Wayne Carter (p. 94) and *Rhondda Leader* newspaper. Also, to everybody I met on my journey to produce this book and who supplied me with useful information, especially Ty Pentwyn Nursing and Residential Home (Treorchy).

There are just a few people I would like to send a special thank you to: my mentor Tracy Pallant for her technical support and words of wisdom; Jane Friel at Tempus Publishing, for her continued patience; Betty Harris and Tessa for driving me to those remote spots of the valley and to you the public for buying this, my first book.

Also a special thank you to Cat and Mike for their continued support throughout the making and editing of this book and to all the staff at Brown Cow Productions, Cardiff. Thank you all.

If you can put a name to a face, have further historical information or wish to make a comment about this book, or to be kept informed of forthcoming ventures, then you can contact the author, Sean James Cameron, via e-mail address: sean_james_cameron@hotmail.com.

Literal English translations of Welsh place names have been added in brackets on first mention.

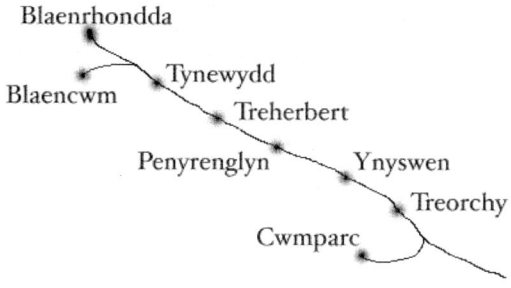

A map showing the Rhondda communities.

INTRODUCTION

The villages covered in this book lie among mountainous and picturesque scenery at the foot of Pen Pych (*mountain top*) mountain, which rises one thousand seven hundred feet above sea level. It is eleven miles north-west from Pontypridd (*bridge of the earthen house*) and is the 'end-of-the-line' of the Valleys Railway service.

An early nineteenth century tourist described the area as a 'truly picturesque district which has been called the Alps of Glamorgan; where the rocks and glens, steep precipices and mountain streams, which occur perpetually between Bwlch-y-Clawdd (*pass of the mountain*), Cwmsaerbren (*woodland valley*) and Blaenrhondda (*head of the Rhondda*), would no longer be neglected by a tourist fond of grand objects'.

The shape of the hills, the courses of streams and waterfalls are as they have been for centuries. Even today the magnificence of Cwmsaerbren Basin, the charm of dingle-dells and waterfalls at Blaencwm (*head of the valley*) remain a testimony to the natural beauty of the Upper Rhondda. Until the middle nineteenth century, the area lay completely off the beaten track, at the head of a secluded pastoral valley which had preserved all the characteristics of rural charm.

The history of the area can be dated as far back as the thirteenth century when the first recorded people lived on the mountain tops overlooking Blaenrhondda. Even today the remains of their community can be found as you drive up the Rhigos (*place of heather*) mountain road; parking the car on the boundary of Rhondda and Aberdare the site is just a short walk away. Over the years, nature has covered these remains and a visit is best made during the winter when the stones are more visible, though whatever time of year you visit you will still be able to walk down one of the original streets, used today by forestry vehicles.

In 1800 the Rhondda's population was 542 residents, a stark contrast to today's estimated 60,000. It was during the mid-1800s that the communities of Treherbert and district grew. Chapels, churches, collieries, shops and schools all sprang up creating a picture of commercial and social vitality. In less than 150 years the picture would change. Towards the end of the twentieth century and beginning of the twenty-first, all we see are buildings being destroyed with no replacement. It is little wonder that new generations today are looking outside the valley for a better life. The valley is becoming green once more, coal heaps and winding gear are now tourist attractions. There is still a lot to be done to improve the area but the determination of Rhondda people will win out and the valley will again become a place of promise and opportunity.

General view of Treherbert, 2000.

Chapter 1
BLAENCWM
(HEAD OF THE VALLEY)

Local residents and tourists enjoy a pleasant afternoon in the streams on the mountainside overlooking Blaencwm during the summer of 1996.

Glenrhondda (*Rhondda valley*) Colliery opened its No. 1 pit in 1911 and No. 2 pit in 1921 both by the Glenavon Garw Colliery Company, employing 230 men. Closed in September 1966 by the National Coal Board the 321 miners were transferred to other local pits or retired. After the closure 54 men remained at the colliery until the whole site was cleared. During the late 1990s the entrance to the shaft caved-in, exposing the dark hole that would have carried the pits cage. Now the area has been landscaped and the only visible sign of the pit is a mound of concrete and surrounding protection fence.

The Rhondda and Swansea Bay Railway line leading to Tynewydd (*new house*) in 1958. On the right hand side of the railway is Glenrhondda (*Rhondda valley*) Colliery and coal screen. During the early 1990s a land reclamation scheme transformed the area into attractive streams and walkways. Glenrhondda Colliery was also known as the 'Hook and Eye'. There are two differing explanations for this title, the first being that when colliers from other nearby collieries were reputedly told to 'sling their hook' they would go to Glenrhondda to see if they could 'eye up' any work. The other explanation is that one of the old foremen had an accident and his hand was replaced with a hook and one of his eyes was made of glass. If you wanted work at the colliery you went and spoke to 'hook and eye'.

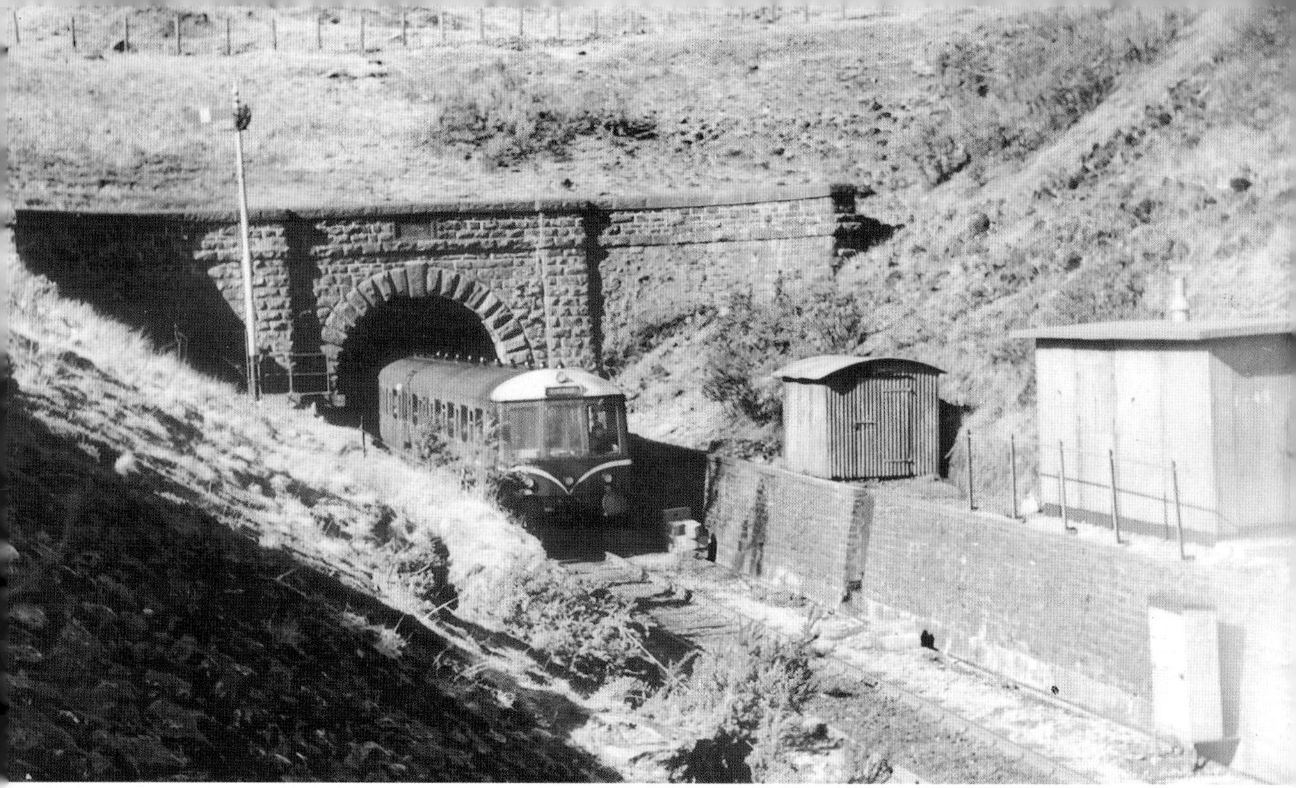

One of the last diesel trains to leave Blaencwm Tunnel heading for Blaenrhondda station from Blaengwnfi (*source of the river Gwnfi*) during 1958. Work commenced on the tunnel in June 1885 and it was to measure 3,300yds, becoming the seventh longest tunnel in the United Kingdom. Workmen on both sides of the mountain began work and met in the middle. Passengers described the tunnel as being in a near straight line except for a slight kink in the middle. This was in the days before laser guided digging, and according to one local resident when the tunnel workers met in the middle they had to dig out a large dome in order to connect both ends. When the steam trains were approaching Blaencwm, you could see their steam coming out of a vent halfway up the mountainside. Under the Dr Beeching railway plans, the tunnel was closed in 1963. The tunnel lies 20ft below the earth and today the only sign of its existence is a manhole cover. Follow the direction of the three trees in the centre of today's picture and the tunnel cover can be found directly below.

Blaencwm signal box in 1958. Today it isimpossible to imagine Blaencwm during its early years. Coal mines and railways have all been removed and the village is now one of the most attractive places to live in the Rhondda, attracting many tourists from all over the world during its Summer months. The mountains are home to many species of wildlife including kestrels, mink and herons. Tourists have been known to compare its mountains to those of the Alps.

A steam train races through Blaencwm on its way to Blaengwnfi during 1900. Note the lack of houses and colliery. The row of houses just to the right of the train's steam, Glanselsig (*bank of the river Selsig*) Terrace, was completed in 1865. During that April two houses were used for fellowship worship and the first baptism took place in June of that year, at the nearby river. The baptism was conducted by the Revd W. Jenkins, Minister of Libanus Chapel. The railway bridge was removed in 1943 and a year later, on Sunday 20 February, a sixty-one-year-old man, Thomas John (formerly of Taff's Well), died when he stumbled over the edge of one of its buttresses, falling onto the road below. John, was reported to have been in a 'quarrelsome mood and had been drinking' and was looking for a place to sleep. During the previous evening he was seen at Treherbert asking for directions to the colliery. The inquest noted that there was only one barrier on one of the buttresses and suggested to the colliery manager that, 'it is advisable to have a barrier placed on both sides'. No action was taken against the colliery.

Opened in 1923 the Glenrhondda Colliery Workmen's Institute was home to many local groups and societies. They included the Glenrhondda Operatic Society who performed their first production *Maritana* on 23 November 1948 with David Williams as producer and Gwladys Jenkins as pianist, Mr W.J. Richards as musical director along with official, chairman Jess Williams and secretary Jack Morgan of Tynewydd. The building was demolished during the late 1960s and replaced by a private residence.

Situated at the top of Hendrewen (*white winter dwelling*) Street is Glenrhondda Colliery (steam coal seams). Upon entering Blaencwm you are greeted by the allotments where gardeners such as Rodrick and Pickens attend their fruit and vegetables for exhibiting at the local Treherbert and District Gardening Society shows. During the early 1990s these allotments were part of the Blaencwm-in-Bloom competition. The whole community took part by displaying window boxes and hanging baskets outside their houses and this has now become an annual event.

Llyngwyn Road, 1987 (above). Extensive work was carried out on the Tynewydd to Blaencwm railway line during 1995, with all the railway bridges being removed and surrounding areas landscaped. Today, a two mile walk is possible by following this new bridle path from the head of Blaencwm to behind Tynewydd Square. On the left of the bridge is a public footpath leading into Blaenrhondda. Hardly ever used, the path became overgrown with brambles and was notoriously used by local teenagers for secret activities!

Chapter 2
BLAENRHONDDA
(HEAD OF THE RHONDDA)

Blaenrhondda Colliery (steam coal seams) opened in 1869 and was owned by the Cardiff and Merthyr Steam Coal Company. It closed in July 1978 and the site was later developed during 1987 into 'Western World', a cowboy tourist town which closed a month after opening. During the late 1990s there were many plans for redevelopment such as a dry ski slope, hotels and vast lakes but once again due to lack of finance the plans were shelved. Now the site is having its remaining coal heaps removed in preparation for redevelopment.

Prior to the majority of Blaenrhondda streets becoming grade listed by CADW (*to keep*), one of the original community streets was Cross Brook Street; built to house the influx of miners to the local collieries. It is said that there were so many miners in the Rhondda during its peak that landladies would double book their rooms. During the day one miner would sleep in his bed and when he went off to work the night shift, his pal who was finishing his day shift would use his friend's bed to sleep in. It is said that no bed became cold during the coal rush years.

Blaenrhondda Park, 1950 (below), before the pavilion was built, which was as busy then as it is today. The area is used for many sports such as bowling, rugby, school sports days and football, making the pavilion an important part of community life. Fernhill houses can be seen at the top right of the picture. During January 1972 the residents were moved to the newly-completed Bryn Henllan council housing estate following plagues of rats and problems with installing electric and gas supplies at Fernhill.

Pupils of Blaenrhondda Junior School pose during 1910 for their school photograph. Within a hundred years the school would cease to be used. During the Summer of 1999 the schools of Blaenrhondda, Blaencwm and Tynewydd closed and a purpose-built school was opened on 7 June 1999, on the former site of No. 1 pit at the foot of Pen Pych mountain. Named after the mountain, Pen Pych Community Primary School is under the direction of headmaster Gareth Todd-Jones. The school accommodates 56 infants and 173 juniors with an average attendance of 91.52% and employs 8 teachers.

Here Pen Pych pupils pose for their St David's Day 2001 photograph. Left to right, back row: Shaun Lewis, Joshua Jones, John Stone, Leon Lewis, Thomas Hughes, Patrick Rees, Ryain Waite, Corey Watkins. Middle row: Emily Guy, Levi Matthews, Caitlin Stevens, Charlotte Parry, Ffion Dobbs, Chloé Bury, Cody Llewellyn, Zoé Lewis, Josie Powell. Front row: David Davies, Adam Jones, Cory Williams, Lloyd Shankland, Lloyd Warren, Brandon Lewis, Connor Swain, Tyrone Evans.

On 18 September 1921 there was great excitement when a balloon was spotted coming down over Blaenrhondda. The balloon, along with its Spanish competitors, was taking part in the Gordon-Bennett International Balloon Race and was blown off course landing near Fernhill Colliery. The nearby war memorial which can be found in Clyngwyn Road was erected during the 1920s to commemorate those who gave their lives in the First World War.

Pen Pych (*the Sentinel*) mountain is reputed to be the only three-sided flat top mountain in the world! The white building on the right hand side (above) is Glyn Gwyn (*blessed valley*) Farm in 1938.

Chapter 3
TYNEWYDD
(NEW HOUSE)

The 'Moonshiners' of 1925. Left to right, back row: Albert Williams, Wall Watts, Kid Watkins, Emlyn Jones, Mor Evans, -?-, Tom Harris, ? Williams. Middle row: ? Brown, Levi Baynham, Jack Rees, Ben Nicholas, Ivor Watts, Dai Rodrick Evans, Mat Francis. Front row: Dai Griffiths, Vince Hillings, Trevor Rodrick, Eddy Mason, Howell Williams. The Moonshiners were a group of local men who met almost every night in one of the nearby institutes to discuss issues of the day.

View of Tynewydd showing Blaenrhondda station and St Albans Church. The land in front of the station was previously known as Eileen Park, where many games of cricket, football and rugby were played prior to the factory being built in 1947. The factory, Stelco Hardy, manufactured welded stainless steel tubes.

Fernhill Workmen's Institute and Hall, Tynewydd, 1960, locally known as 'The Palace'. When the venue burned down on Monday 25 March 1985 between 5pm and 10pm, it was supposedly offered to the Selsig Amateur Operatic Society for £1, but due to the extensive work required to rebuild the structure, the offer was declined. The building was later demolished and replaced by twelve flats named Hendreselsig (*winter dwelling of the selsig*).

Street leading from Ty Draw (*house yonder*) Terrace to St Albans Terrace. The bridge was demolished as part of the land reclamation scheme which took place between September 1994 and March 1995. The windows of St Albans church are boarded up to protect its stained glass windows.

Blaenrhondda station, with its wooden platform, was the last stop before leaving the valley for Blaengwnfi on the Rhondda and Swansea Bay Line. Near the base of Pen Pych mountain was the home of a travelling blacksmith, and to inform the nearby farms that he was in the area he would raise a flag on a pole outside the building. The remains of the building's foundations are still visible beneath the grass and it is possible to see the air cavity that let heat travel around the building.

Betty Harris recreates the pose taken when she was sixteen (above), showing the view down Halifax Terrace and its changes. Before local resident, Ron Pritchard, constructed his prefab home, the land was being used as a coal merchants yard owned by Mr Denby.

Tynewydd Rugby team (below), date unknown. Left to right, back row: Elwyn Evans, Andrew Davies, Ching Edwards, Ron Broom, Will Morris, Mor Evans, -?-, -?-. Middle row: Dai Jones, Haydon Davies, Binki Williams, Tom Harris, Lucher ?, Walter Blatchford, ? Thomas. Front row: Will Heart, ? Williams, Ibe Rees, Ivor Yearsly, -?-, -?-.

Today the area's most well-known rugby team is based at Treherbert Rugby Club on Wyndham Street and their games are played on the pitch at Tynewydd Park. Pictured second from the left, middle row, is Mr Gwyn Rees.

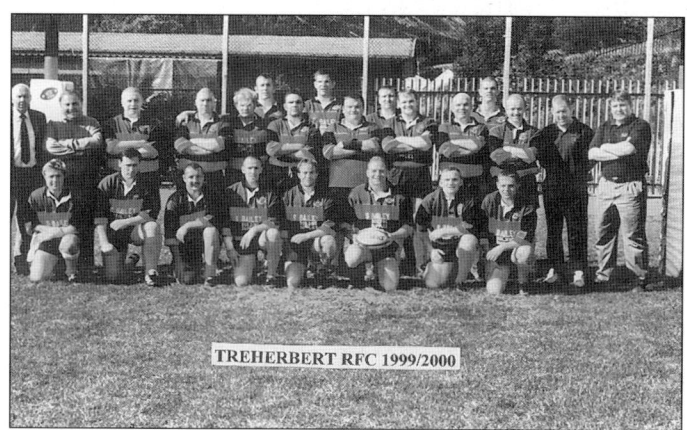

TREHERBERT RFC 1999/2000

Halifax Terrace (above), date unknown, showing Blaencwm Chapel. Next to the chapel was an Italian café with a fish and chip shop next to it.

On 29 September 1866 Thomas Joseph applied to the Dunraven Estate to build a chapel in Tynewydd. Subsequently a lease was granted for ninety-nine years at a rent of £3 3s 0d per annum. The chapel members first met at No. 1 and 2 Chapel Row, Blaencwm, in November 1866, which was blessed by the Revd J. Lloyd Ebenezer of Merthyr. The first communion took place in February 1867 and was taken by Revd Owen of Rhyl. In June Henry Jones and John Lawrence were made the first two chapel deacons. It was on 15 June 1868 that a special service of dedication was held to mark the forming of the newly-built Blaencwm Chapel. Membership was as high as 285 during 1888 but within a year it decreased to 199. During 1889 the chapel closed due to a membership split and it was not until 1 December 1890 that services returned with a membership of 160 under the direction of Revd Mr Hopkins. Today, the members meet in the vestry, only using the chapel for special occasions. One of its members is a Rhondda Assembly Member to the National Assembly of Wales, Mr Geraint Davies, who was elected to office on 7 May 1999.

A view overlooking Tynewydd during 1945 (below). Tynewydd Colliery was opened in 1865 by Ebenezer Lewis, owner of Bwllfa Dare Colliery in Aberdare, and was the first lease of 'mineral land' to be purchased in the Rhondda. A total of 25,000 tons of coal was raised the following year. Two years later the mine was sold for £50,000 to the Rhondda Merthyr Colliery Company and the original founder, Ebenezer Lewis, was appointed managing director. Coal production was put on hold in 1879 when it was discovered that the mine had a serious geological fault. It was not until 1887 that the fault was solved and mining began again under the ownership of Messrs L. and H. Gueret. It is a mystery why the mine was closed in 1911 when only a year earlier it had produced 100,000 tons of coal. The land was redeveloped in 1963 for public enjoyment in the form of children's playground and the playing fields that are home to Treherbert Rugby Football Club.

The original Tynewydd club first began in 1913 at No. 5 Gwendoline Street, (now a private residence). During 1923 the members raised enough funds to purchase a house where the building stands today. The club proved to be a popular meeting place for local people and it was decided to build a 'new hall' extension during 1933.

The club is home to many local performers and during the Christmas festivities is used for 'Carols by Candlelight', organized by the local Cancer Care charity.

Street parties have always been a favourite of Rhondda people and a way of bringing the community together. Here we see (below) the residents of Halifax Terrace, Tynewydd, celebrating VE Day. Left to right: Mr Watts, Mrs Watts, Mrs Barnes, Mrs Iris Harris, Mrs Price, Madeline Lewis, Mrs Nash, Vivian Gallaway, May Purdel, Mr Lewis (wearing a cap).

Fifty years on and the residents of Eleanor Street, Penyrenglyn, celebrate the anniversary of VE Day with food cooked by the wives and tables and chairs on loan from Carmel Chapel. Left to right, back row: ? Fletcher, Cheryl Evans, Elisha Fletcher, Alan Walters (wearing a cap), Phillips Walters, John Dee, Sean James Cameron, Lilian Hole, -?-, Christine ?, Muriel Evans (by gate). Second row: Dafydd Evans, Thomas Evans, ? Hole,

Eleanor Walters holding Remer Walters, Kathrin Edwards, Diane Lewis (*née* Frost) holding Amy Lewis, Megan Green. Front row: Alison Dee, Shasha Walters, Francis Walter, Frankesica Walters, Ann Walters, Margaret Williams, Diane Dee.

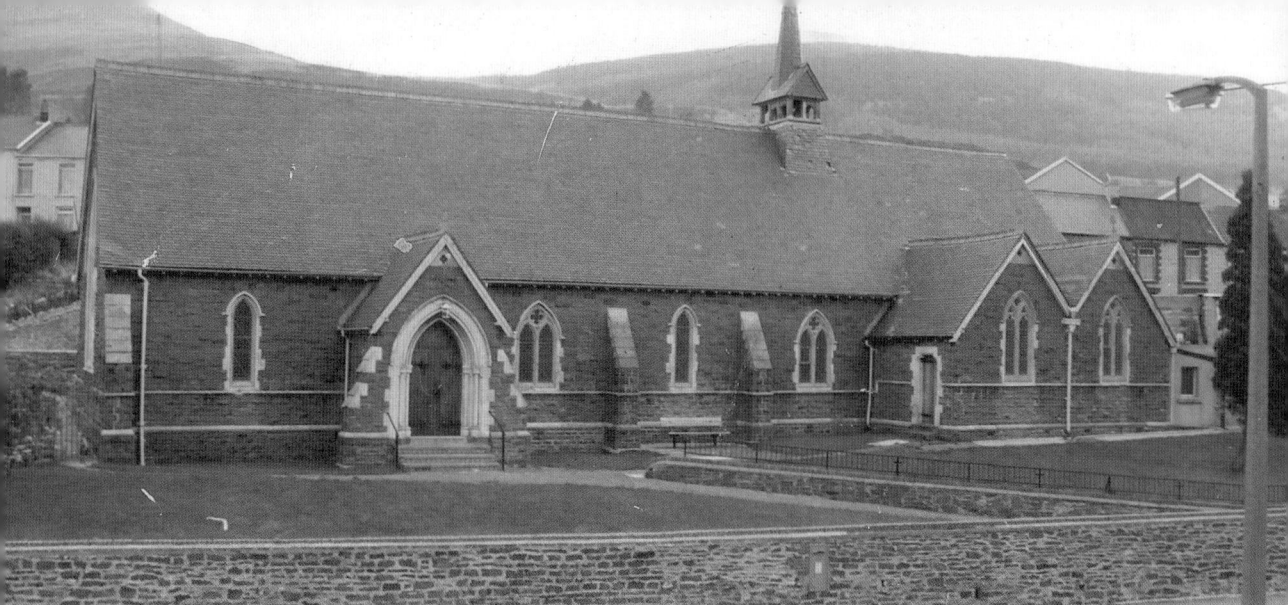

St Albans church, Tynewydd. During the late nineteenth century, village worship was mainly conducted at St Mary's church, Treherbert, but with the sinking of the pits further up the valley there was a call by residents of Blaenrhondda and Tynewydd to construct a new place of worship. A Church Building Committee was established at Dunraven School and at first there was a difference of opinion as to the location of the new church. Many felt that Blaenrhondda would make a suitable home, whereas others opted for Tynewydd. After much discussion Tynewydd, in the shadow of Pen Pych mountain, was decided upon; the land at the junction of Blaencwm and Blaenrhondda. Situated opposite Blaenrhondda railway station the new church, with seating for 331 worshippers and built at a cost of £1,942, was opened and consecrated on Monday 8 November 1891 by Lord Bishop of the Diocese. The Church Building Committee, who signed the Petition for Consecration, were: William Lewis (vicar), Edwin William Lewis and Alban Jones (wardens), William Glass, Frederick James Hockady, Charles Boucher, Frederick Hughes, Frederick Werrel, George Ricketts, John Pratt, Edward Harry and Joseph Thompson.

The creation of this new church symbolized the formation of Treherbert as a separate parish from Ystradyfodwg. With the licence for marriages being presented on Wednesday 24 November that year the first wedding was performed by Revd Lewis. Patronage was made on Sunday 20 February and Monday 19 December the following year and the assignment of a district chapelry to the church was appointed on Wednesday 8 March 1893 with the Revd John Rees as perpetual curate.

A house at the National School on Mount Libanus Street, Penyrenglyn, was used to house the vicar until 1897 when the vicarage, situated at the head of Vicarage Hill in Penyrenglyn, was completed at a cost of £1,396 12s 0d. This building served the church until 1995 when it was sold to help church funds to repair St Matthew's in Treorchy. After many months of searching, a new vicarage was established at Gwendoline Street Tynewydd.

It is recorded that during 1901 St Albans had eighty-five adult members with a Sunday School of ninety-nine children under fifteen years old and twenty-five children aged fifteen to eighteen years old. The teachers were Revd James Davies, Mrs Duke, Janetta Pratt, May Practt, C. Oates, M. Carpenter and Mr Thomas Brokenbrow who also worked as stationmaster at Blaenrhondda railway station. It wasn't until 1914 that St Albans installed its pipe organ, prior to this a harmonium was used.

Bringing the history up-to-date the church sadly held its last service under the direction of Revd Reney. Since its final service the building has remained empty and has come under attack by vandals. The stained-glass windows were covered for protection (see p. 28). During the year 2000 the church committee are awaiting a suitable buyer.

Theatre has played a major role in community life whether it be the local school children celebrating the 'Festival of Britain' in 1951 (May 29 to July 7) (right) or by the members of the Selsig Amateur Operatic Society posing for their 1992 production of *Desert Song*. Both productions were performed at the Parc and Dare Theatre, Treorchy Festival of Britain. Left to right: Edward Gregory, Malcom Jenkins, Iris Davies, David Quelch, Joan Rees, Bryan ?, ? Bowen, Gwyn ?, -?-, Betty Harris, Bryan True (kneeling), Marian Riley. Costumes and sets were all hand-made by the children. Actor Donald Houston and his brother paid a visit to a Treherbert school to see rehearsals in progress and were so impressed that they wanted to take the whole concert to the West End. Due to the number of children that took part from three nearby schools and the difficulty of transporting them to London, the plans were shelved. Participating in *Desert Song* are, left to right: -?-, Don Morgan, Robert Medcraft, Geraint Evans, Margaret Evans, Glen Bowen, -?-.

A view looking up to Tynewydd from the mountainside behind Treherbert Hospital (above). Allotment sites still occupy space in the modern view today.

Chapter 4
Treherbert
(The Three Herberts)

On Sunday 6 September 1857 a dispute began between two Welsh and Irish colliery workers at the Bute Arms in Treherbert Square, but no more than words were exchanged. The next day a fight broke out in the square between the two men and the Irish collier was the winner, who then downed a pint at the Bute Arms before heading home with pals. This was the final straw for the Treherbert colliers and on the Tuesday morning several hundred men marched to the homes of the Irish families and ordered them to 'quit the village'. The Irish ignored the warning and, that evening, the local men marched back to the Irish homes with sticks and stones. Doors and windows of eight Irishmen's homes were smashed to pieces and as the Welsh drove the Irish down the valley they used their weapons to break arms and heads until they had driven them out of the valley. The Irish women and children were allowed to escape unharmed. With their work done the Welsh returned to Treherbert Square and the Bute Arms (known today as the Marquis of Bute) for a pint or two! When the police, headed by Superintendent Thomas, were seen heading up the road to the pub the attackers quickly dispersed and returned home ... where of course they had been 'for the entire evening!'

The English Wesleyan Methodist church was built in 1884 and was demolished in February 1987. A new church building was erected that year together with Glenrhondda Court next door which is a residence for the elderly, and was officially opened by HM Queen Elizabeth II.

The Treherbert junction leading up Dunraven Street to the left and Abertonllwyd Street to the right which now leads onto the Rhigos mountain road passing Tynewydd Park and Rugby field. Before the introduction of the tramcar in September 1908 the only mode of transport was the horse and cart. One quiet winter's evening a horse wandering around Treherbert, believed to be on its way to Tynewydd, slipped on the ice covered road and fell to the ground at the corner of Abertonllwyd Street, dying on impact. A policeman was on his beat at the time and witnessed the incident; he called to a passing boy to assist him … ('otherwise he would start asking questions about the bag of coal that the boy was discreetly hiding behind his back!'). The policeman began to write down what had happened until he came to the street name. He was an Englishman, only recently posted to Treherbert, and wanted to make a good impression with his first case but he found that he couldn't spell the street name: Abertonllwyd or as it was spelt then, Abartonllwyd Street. Not wanting to look foolish in front of the young boy and unable to find a street sign he ordered the boy to help him drag the horse over the ice and into nearby Hill Street. A few minutes later the policeman's statement read that the 'horse fell and died in Hill Street' thus impressing his colleagues on completing his first case!

S taff workers of the Co-operative Stores pose outside their place of work in 1910. Today the building is called Abertonllwyd Flats, with accommodation for thirteen residents.

The foundation stones of Treherbert Hospital were laid on 19 April 1927 by the Chairman of the Hospital Committee, Mr Trefor L. Mort ME JP, and the hospital was officially opened on 7 December of that year. As local residents and officials celebrated the opening on the hospital steps, little did they know that within seventy-five years the hospital would be demolished. After a long and bitter fight, Treherbert residents lost their battle to save the hospital, and on 11 December 1999 the doors were finally closed and the hospital was later demolished. Remaining patients were transferred to the nearby George Thomas Hospital at Treorchy. During 2000 the local authority received an application to build ten detached homes with adjoining garages on the site.

Leading from the Aberdare valley to Treherbert, the Rhigos mountain road, or as it's known locally 'the new road', was constructed after 1908 and is often closed during the winter due to heavy snow falls. From 1935 the area was heavily planted with fir trees to supply the growing number of mines that were in the area: their trunks being used as pit props. Many of the valley's landmarks have vanished, such as the Baglan Field coal tip (centre right) and St Mary's church (right). St Mary's Close where local chemist and the first National Assembly of Wales member for the Rhondda, Geraint Davies resides, now occupies the site. The Baglan Field coal tip was flattened by local residents during the early 1970s.

Music has always been a part of Treherbert and one of the most memorable groups was the Treherbert Jazz Band known as 'The Green and White Star and Crescent'. Here the committee stands on the steps of Treherbert Hospital during 1952. Today, Treherbert Silver Band, who practise in the band room on Taff Street, is one of the leading silver bands in the Rhondda, winning prizes all over the world. On the right, back row, is the late John Henry Landon Thomas, 'Jack'.

View across the valley from the Rhigos mountain showing Mynydd Tyle Coch (*mountain of the red brick*). Above St Mary's church (bottom centre) is Lady Margaret Colliery (steam coal seams) which was sunk in 1877 and owned by the Marquis of Bute. During 1923 and 1924 there was an unexpected increase in demand for coal and the population of Rhondda peaked at 167,485 the largest population ever known in Rhondda. The coal boom was not to last however and it collapsed during the winter of 1924. The mine closed in 1929, but was used for maintenance purposes long after nationalization in 1947.

Situated at the end of Station Street is the Rhondda Valley Brewery and in 1901 its secretary was George A. Foote. A hay merchant and dealer business was located where Treherbert swimming pool now stands and in front of the Lady Margaret Colliery is a sports field, now the site of Everest Limited which opened around 1975.

Treherbert outdoor swimming baths during the Summer of 1924 (below). Top left is the Bute Colliery (steam coal seam) sunk between 1850 and 1855 by the Marquis of Bute and closed in 1926. Set in the grounds of Jubilee Park, the baths were demolished at the end of Summer 1992 and reopened in November 1995 as an indoor all-year-round swimming pool with retractable roof. Local schools use the baths for swimming lessons and many local children have achieved medals for their swimming. Pen Pych mountain stands proudly at the head of the valley.

A general view of Treherbert, 1936 (above). Opened in 1899, Treherbert Infants School (centre) now accommodates approximately ninety-six children aged three to seven years with an average attendance of 80%, and has development links with local and international projects. Its chair of governors is Mrs Dona Sarsby, deputy headteacher Mrs Elizabeth Davies and headteacher Mrs Jill Evans. As well as over twenty-five years service at the school, Mrs Evans is also a well-known figure in the community for her involvement with the local amateur operatic society, Selsig, and has been an active committee member and leading-lady for the organization for many years. Note in the modern photograph that Treherbert Hospital has now been demolished (top right).

Station Street during 1900 was a very different street from the one we know today. There were many shops: booksellers, grocers, greengrocers, shoemakers, a pub and a public hall better known as the 'Opera House'. Erected in 1872 at a cost of £2,500, with a seating capacity of 1,000, the Opera House was paid for by funds raised from concerts held at Carmel and Libanus chapels under the direction of Mr M.O. Jones. Its stage was so strong it once held an elephant. Following the First World War the popularity of the Opera House declined. One night the hall was crowded and local singer Todd-Jones was to perform, but he was next door in the Railway Inn, drinking. They forcibly carried him to the Opera House and led him to the stage. Tom 'the Co-op' Davies, was his instructor and pianist. Todd-Jones would not study music but followed the pianist in song, he sang *Machwshia* and the response was terrific. This performance is claimed to have been the last 'great' event at the Opera House. It was sadly destroyed by a fire in 1934 and if rumours are to be believed, it was deliberately set ablaze so that a fight between two local husbands didn't take place on its stage. One of the wives, fearing her husband would be killed by the other man, went to the theatre under the cover of darkness and set the building alight. Whether or not the fight took place at another venue is unknown. During February 1912 the stage was taken over by the Treherbert Operatic Society who performed *HMS Pinafore*; this is the only known mention of a Treherbert Operatic Society.

R.T. Jones Ironmongers, Sheffield House, Bute Street is now the home of the Rhondda Borough Council Area Office. Situated opposite the Bute Reading Room, now known as St Mary's Schoolroom, the ironmongers shop was later turned into a café/tea room by his wife, Catherine Jones. Later still, her two daughters turned it into a sweet shop with a boys club and dance hall at the back of the building. The venue was struck by a fire a few years later that destroyed the boys club.

St Mary's Church was built in 1868, costing £4,000. At the same time the Marquees of Bute, aged twenty-one, married into the family of the Duke of Norfolk and was admitted into the Roman Catholic Church. Being a Roman Catholic he was unwilling to convert the church to the Ecclesiastical Commissioners. The church was licensed on 4 September 1868 as a Chapel of Ease with William Morgan as vicar and Jones Price as curate. St Mary's church was opened for Public Worship four days later on 8 September 1868. The church experienced many structural problems and was deemed unsafe, and demolished in 1967, one year short of its centenary. This site is now occupied by St Mary's Close and some allotments. Remains of the original building can still be found on the site.

Just above the phone box in Bute Street (on the right in modern picture) is Treherbert Library which was converted from a chapel, known as 'Sticky Chapel'. When the chapel pews were varnished one summer they didn't dry in time for the Sunday service and when the congregation rose to sing the first hymn, they couldn't get up because their clothes were stuck to the seats.

On the right is the Gaiety Cinema now a Spar store run by Michael Pritchard. The cinema was a source of relief for residents, an opportunity to escape into the fantasy world of cowboys and indians and romantic lovers. During its time the cinema was visited by famous stars, including Charlie Chaplain, who delighted crowds with his famous walk, cane and hat. The opening date of the cinema is unknown but it was demolished in 1970. The Grand Theatre in Pentre was demolished in the same year.

Treherbert railway station can be found at the foot of Cwmsaerbren Basin. The line was operated by the Taff Vale Railway and was opened on 7 August 1856 for mineral service, and it was not until 7 January 1863 that the first passenger service began. The carriages were exceedingly primitive; a third class carriage was more like a horse-box. There were long seats the length of the window-less carriage, and the only ventilation was through a latticed aperture. Doors were locked just prior to leaving the station and at the next station the doors were opened by the guard, and then closed again. In July 1880 the first Rhondda and Swansea Bay Railway service for minerals and passengers began. Today the station only has one track leading from Treherbert to Cardiff and beyond. 'Sprinter' trains can now be seen making the £3.80 return trip to Cardiff. The future of the station is under threat with so many commuters now choosing to use their

cars and gone are the days when the platform was filled to capacity by the members of local chapels and societies on their annual away days.

During the latter part of the twentieth century an organization was formed to recreate railway heritage and to reopen a traditional 'steam' line between Treherbert and Blaencwm. Due to problems with land stability the project was abandoned during the Spring of 2000.

Peglars Store, Bute Street is now home to David Rees solicitors, although the 'Peglars' stone sign can still be seen when entering the establishment. Here Mr Peglar is serving a customer who has purchased the first electric radio to be sold in the valley. A local celebrities today is Kevin Mason or as he is better known 'Kevin the Milk' (below). Kevin has been involved with many television programmes, he played himself in the BBC Wales drama *A Light In The Valley* and appeared on BBC 1's *Ground Force* with Alan Titchmarsh, Charlie Dimmock and Tommy Walsh. Kevin sold his milk round in Easter 2000 to Mr Ashley Lewis of Brook Street Blaenrhondda and continued to work with him until November of that year.

Built in 1871 Treherbert police station (below) served the local community until it was closed and demolished in 1967 to make way for council accommodation known as Ty Heddlu (*police house*) (see p. 41).

Family life in the valley has changed over the years. Due to the increased threat of family deaths through coal mine related illnesses and accidents, many families would have had as many as twelve children. Here we see a typical large family gathering (below) and an example of one of today's smaller ones. The Howell family are seen in 1932 and the modern family is represented by Alyson Williams and baby Anya Violet Williams, aged nine months, seen in 2000 .

> # WARD I
> ## Joint Residents' Association
> (Tynewydd, Treherbert, Penyrenglyn)
>
> ---
>
> # REPORT OF MEETING
>
> with
>
> ## Mr. A. RIGBY
> ### DESIGN PARTNERSHIP
>
> # PLAN Rhondda 2001
>
> ---
>
> PRICE - ONE SHILLING

During the summer of 1969 the local authority issued their plans for re-developing the Upper Rhondda for the twenty-first century. Many parts of their plan have been introduced, includng road bypasses. However, the plans caused huge public protest at the time and objection was raised to ideas such as the demolishing of Hendrewen Road Blaencwm, Station Street Treherbert, Bute Street Treherbert, Eleanor Street and Baglan Street Penyrenglyn; plus the replacement of the railway with a bypass road. Due to the pressure of local action groups and residents many of the council's plans were shelved.

The 'Green and White Star and Crescent' band (see p. 45) in 1950 marching on the Baglan Field. The street on the left is Oak Street with the Corner House pub towards the end of the street. The building on the right is Dutfields Store, which had the same owner as 'Olivers' shop a little higher up (see p. 63). Dutfields draper/outfitters/ post office and general store was destroyed by a fire during the 1950s. A cyclist on his way to Treherbert noticed smoke coming out of one of the windows and alerted the fire brigade but it was too late. The double fronted building was later demolished.

Chapter 5
PENYRENGLYN
(HOME OF THE ANGEL)

Treherbert from Penyrenglyn.

A view of Penyrenglyn (above) looking towards Treherbert, taken from the top of the Baglan Field coal tip, which was removed between 1971 and 1972. The street directly under the oak tree in the middle right is River Row, where a travelling fair would set up its carousel. River Row lay on the boundary of Treherbert and Penyrenglyn.

This aerial view of the valley from Ynyswen (*pleasant meadow*) to Tynewydd was taken in 1902 and shows how much the area has been developed over the last one hundred years. Communities such as Tynewydd, Treherbert and Penyrenglyn were well established at the turn of the nineteenth century but as we can see the community of Ynyswen, right, is relatively new. During the early part of the twentieth century, Ynyswen, was seen as a bridge between Penyrenglyn and Treorchy. It was not until the end of the century that it started to create its own community with the development of its industrial sites, health clinic, village hall and many more streets.

Looking down Baglan Street (above) at the junction of Eleanor Street and Mary Street in the days of the tramcar. At the entrance to Eleanor Street on the right hand side is the Welcome Inn. In 1851 it was run by 'Sanders Bach' who was a great supporter of Penyrenglyn Rugby Club and never missed a match.

During 1901 the street had seven shops: two butchers, two grocers, one drapers, one beer retailer, and a hairdressers as well as Carmel Chapel. Today it only has a grocers, a fish and chip shop, a chapel and a pub. During the Second World War all street signs were melted down to be used for the war effort and it was only in the 1990s that the signs for 'Penyrenglyn' and 'Eleanor Street' were replaced. This picture marks the ward boundary between Treherbert and Penyrenglyn.

The Royal Exchange, 1905. It was by far the largest building in Penyrenglyn. During 1851 it was three storeys high with a number of guest rooms, a special dancing room and plenty of room behind the inn for coaches and horses. It was run by Mr Pearce, who was blind but was a wonderful harpist. In 1882 he won first prize at the Denbigh Eisteddfod. Over the coach house at the back was a large gymnasium for wrestling and boxing that was also used for a weekly scouts club. Mr Pearce Jnr was a schoolmaster. The building began to fall into decay during the war. Now it is owned by Jim and Christine Stuart of Dumfries Street who took over the business on 18 June 1999. Prior to the Stuarts' it was owned by Brian Oliver, son of previous owner Jimmy Oliver, well-known for driving his vintage car around the village. Before the Olivers it was owned by Mr Dutfield who also owned a shop lower

down the street opposite Carmel Chapel (see page 59). Dutfield was an Englishman and had the first car hire service in the valley. From 1895 the Royal Exchange became home for the newly-formed Penyrenglyn Rugby Club also known as the Penyrenglyn All Whites Football Club; they were later based at the Smith Arms, just a few doors away.

Situated at the junction of St Mary's Street, Hopkin Street and Libanus Street, the National School was built by Canon Lewis, who also built the nearby All Saints Church in St Mary's Street. Work on the school commenced in 1861 and it was officially opened on 17 October 1861 by the Bishop of Llandaff, who granted a license and authority for the performance of Divine Service on 1 November of that year. A teachers wage at that time was £1 6s 0d. The photograph above was taken in May 1975 and the building was later bought by Mr Roy Duncan who renovated it into a house before moving to Stuart Street, Treherbert.

Penyrenglyn Junior School was opened in 1911 and can be found in Charles Street. When the school first opened boys and girls were separated but in 1964 the headmaster, Mr Charlie Evans, amalgamated the classes. Today, the school has 168 pupils in 5 mainstream classes and 2 special classes, with 7 teaching staff and a deputy head, all under the direction of its headteacher Mr John Griffiths.

The school has a high record of achievement in many fields of sports and pupils have played as far afield as Scotland. The author of this book attended the school during the 1980s.

Plans for a new purpose-built school on a nearby disused tip were being discussed at the time this book was written. Prior to the school opening local children attended Ynyswen School.

General View, Treherbert.

Pupils of Penyreglyn Infants School pose for their St David's Day group photographs in both pictures. The modern photograph was taken in 2001. Pupils from the nursery and reception group are, left to right, back row: Liam Davies, Adam Wilson, Joshua Collinson, Jason Russell, Eathan Allen, Bryan Richings (holding daffodil). Middle row: Natalie Clarke, Katie Cutter, Danielle Butler, Lauren Thomas, Stacey Bosanko, Shauna Jenkins, Jessica Bethell. Front row: Ben Hughes, Tyler Mengas, Shannan Jones, Cedric the Dragon, Melissa Owens, Alex Wigley, Steven Richings (brother of daffodil holder). The school comprises of three classes and two teachers including headmistress Mrs M.M. Williams. During 2000 there were plans to amalgamate Penyrenglyn Infants and Junior School into one purpose-built school situated on the Baglan Field, plans are currently on going with a provisional opening date of September 2002.

Ynysfeio Colliery during 1910. The colliery was sunk in 1854 by James Thomas of Ynyshir and his partners, Mathew Cope of Cardiff and John Lewis of Aberdare on behalf of the landowners, Troederhiw (*foot of the hill*) Coal Company. Output during 1874 was 36,000 tons, increasing to 102,000 tons in 1877. After nationalization in 1947, 3 men were employed for pumping and maintenance work. The villages of Ynysfeio and Penyrenglyn grew around the colliery and on the right hand side can be seen the formation of the Ynysfeio coal tip, now known as the Baglan Field. This burning tip is impossible to imagine today, as it reached way above the main row of houses and was visible for miles. It was not until the late 1980s that a coal tip opposite the Baglan Field stopped smouldering. Local residents like Ivor Williams fought for many years to keep it an open space but in the late 1990s, it was fenced and is now the playing field for local clubs such as Treherbert Boys Club, Treorchy RFC Young, Tynewydd Hotel Team, and Treorchy RFC.

COLLECTOR-WALES

YNYSFEIO COLLIERY
TREHERBERT
RHONDDA
c1910

COLLECTORCARD
Croydon CR0 1HW

c1299

Ynysfeio Bridge looking towards Ynyswen (top). The date of this photograph is unknown but by studying other pictures of the area we can suggest it was taken prior to the First World War. During 1927 the brick bridge was dismantled and rebuilt in steel, and the road was made wider. The whole bridge was finally taken away in February 1972 with a few of the right hand side bricks being taken to nearby Eleanor Street and used to construct a supporting wall in a large garden at the head of the street. The garden at the time was owned by the Williams family but it changed hands in 1996. Dennis Fletcher, World Champion grower of Chrysanthemums, now works the land as a garden growing produce for exhibiting all over the United Kingdom. Now all that remains (left) is the supporting left hand side wall leading up to the Forest View guest house, owned by Mr Meredith.

Chapter 6
TREORCHY
(HOME OF THE RIVER ORCKWY)

Bridge re-construction in Station Street, Treorchy. A narrow gauge track had to be laid to transport the side girders of the new bridge from the railway station sidings to the scene of operations which can now be found next to 'Station Café'.

The boundary linking Ynyswen to Treorchy, known as Maes-y-Ffrwd (*meadow of the stream*). The railway line was used to transport coal from the nearby Abergorki (*mouth of the river Gorki*) Colliery to the marshalling yards at Tylecoch for distribution. When the colliery closed in April 1938, the crossing was removed and it is said that the gates ended up in a Treherbert back garden. The colliery site was later used for council refuse then developed into a housing complex during the 1980s.

Abergorky Colliery and tips, in 1936, which end behind Ramah Chapel. This is where on 20 July 1947 the first concert of the newly-reformed Treorchy & District Male Choir was held, who later became the Treorchy Male Voice Choir, although they have subsequently changed their name back to Treorchy Male Choir (see p. 81).

Except for the removal of the colliery tips and conversion of the Salvation Army Hall into a garage, we see almost no change to the area. The colliery was sunk in 1863 by J.H. Insole of Cymmer Colliery, Porth, and was closed in 1938.

Before Treorchy Cemetery was opened, burials took place at Libanus Chapel, Treherbert, but a large increase in local population meant that there was a need for a public cemetery. So in 1871 Treorchy Cemetery was opened and Libanus was then only used to bury its members who already had a family grave. Over the years Treorchy Cemetery has grown rapidly with new sections of land needing to be used. People have wondered what will happen when the cemetery fills the mountain, it will perhaps carry on over the mountain and beyond! At the start of the twenty-first century the grounds are managed by Keith Davies, and records show that, including cremated remains, 63,479 people have been buried.

Bute Street, Treorchy. The business on the left, in the old photograph, was a haberdashery, and is now Geraint Davies' chemist, one of the three shops owned by him. The chapel on the right is St Matthew's Church. Prior to becoming a church, the building was used as a National School classroom until 1887 when it was renovated at a cost of £344.

The later photograph was taken outside the Cardiff Arms Hotel where, during the early part of the 1900s, the open spaces in front of the pub and houses were used as a mini-market every Saturday night.

A Rhondda family-run business during 2000. C.J. Morris, butchers, of High Street, Treorchy, has been serving the community since November 1988; the site was previously used by Eddy Lewis of 'Lewis Butchers'. Here father, Cyril Morris is pictured with his son, Jeff, getting ready for another busy day.

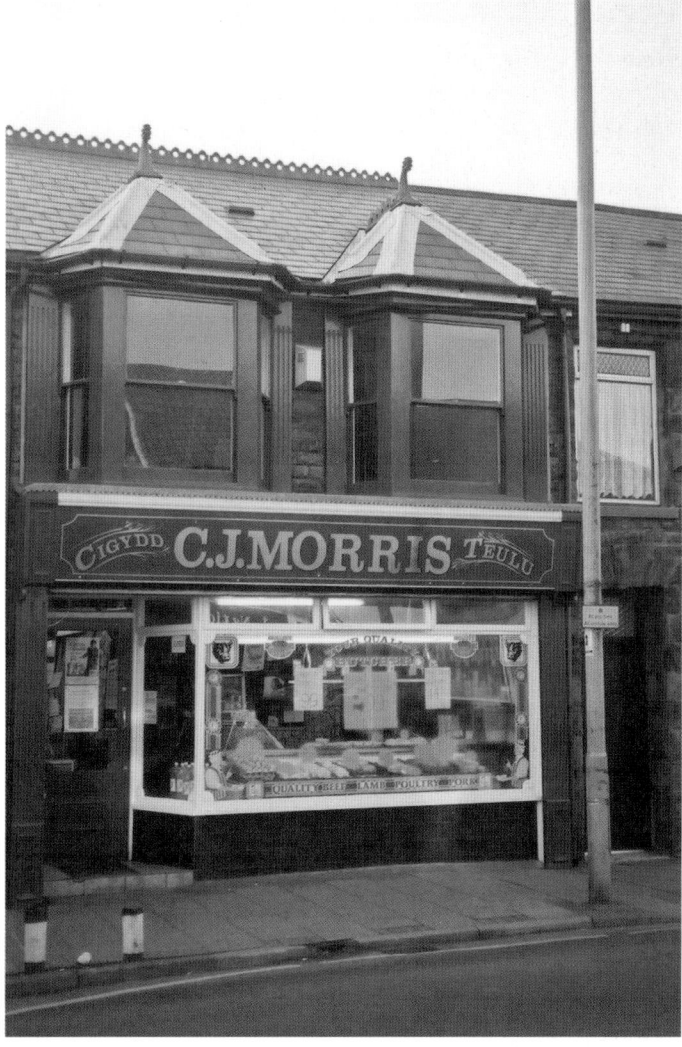

G. Sidoli's confectionery shop on Bute Street was one of the main express cafes in Treorchy. Italian cafes were, and still are, a common site around the valley. Italian families arrived in South Wales during the 1890s from Bardy, Northern Italy, in search of work. They opened coffee shops up and down the valley and were affectionately called 'Bracchi's' after the first immigrants. Today, one of the most popular cafés in Treorchy is 'Carpanini's', opposite the Cardiff Arms pub.

One of the well-known Italian families in the Treorchy area were the Sidoli's. Here Mrs Sidoli and her daughters Gina and Angela are having a quiet five minutes in their busy Express Cafe. They owned the cafe until the mid-1950s. Gina's granddaughter, Lisa, works as a film casting director in America.

Today there are only a few cafés in the area such as Carpanini's. The business was established in 1947 when Mr and Mrs Carpanini arrived in Treorchy from the Italian village of Bardi. Situated opposite the Cardiff Arms public house, the café is run by their children Irene, Francesco, Pietro and Gianmarco (pictured).

Treorchy is as busy a high street today as it was when this photograph was taken. Shops still litter the streets but cars are now a major problem when visiting the area for the weekly shop. These small community shops were once a lifeline for its residents but now they have to compete with large out-of-town stores offering 'all you ever need under one roof'. When these main streets were constructed their width was measured in order to turn a horse and cart around comfortably (a width of 50ft); today the road appears smaller with cars parked each side.

In 1867 Noddfa Chapel stood alone but today it is impossible to recreate the same image due to the growing community of shops over the years. Noddfa was built in 1867 and could seat 1,690 worshippers but in the late 1980s the building was destroyed by a fire that was seen as far away as Pentre and Treherbert. Access through the main street was closed and the local and surrounding communities came to a standstill for many hours.

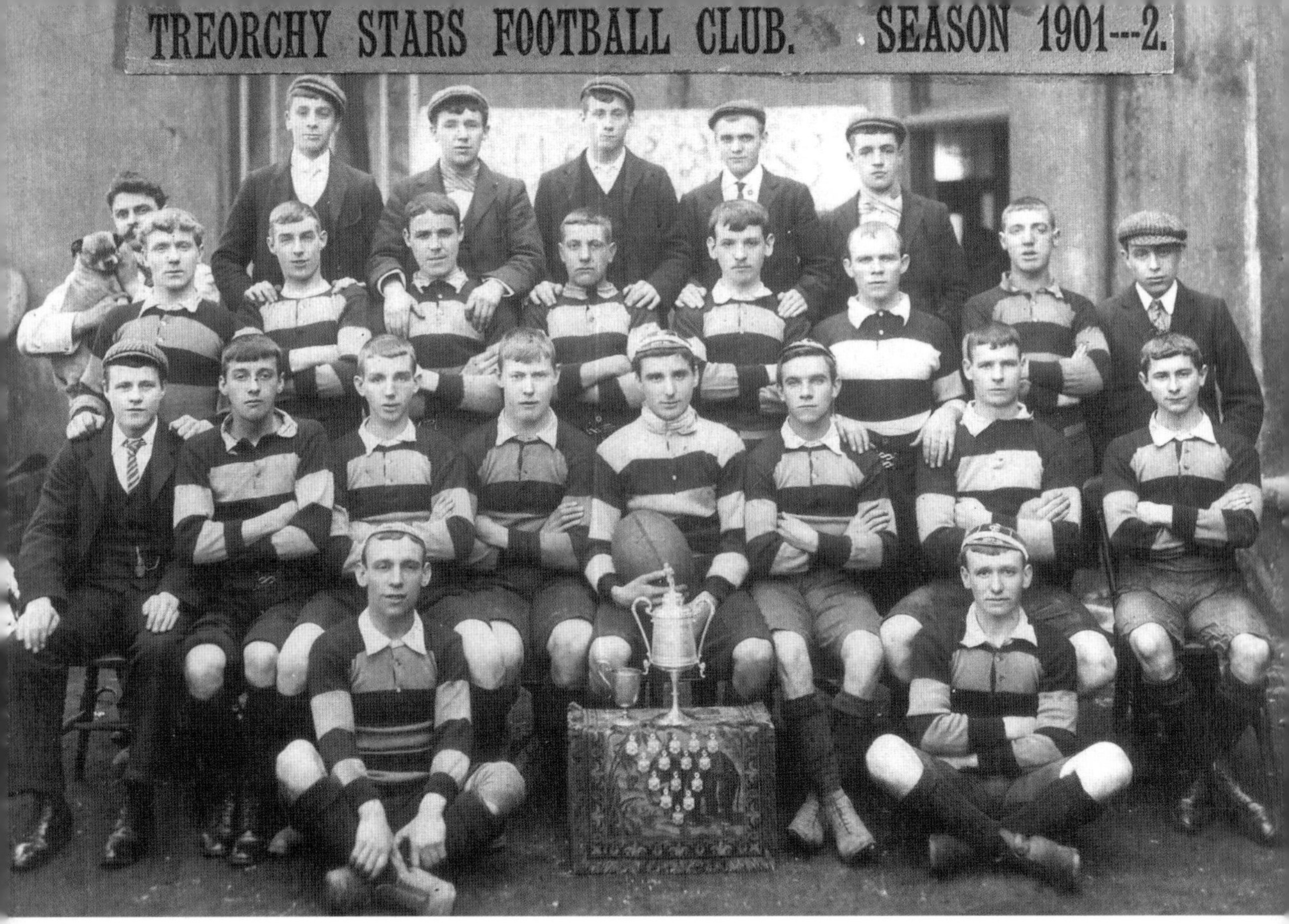

TREORCHY STARS FOOTBALL CLUB.   SEASON 1901---2.

Treorchy Stars Football Club of 1901/02 (above) and the under-15s soccer winners of Treorchy Comprehensive School of 1992. The 1992 team collected the Glamorgan Chairman's Cup with a 7-0 thrashing of Bedwas Comprehensive School in front of an impressed Mr Eddy May, manager of Cardiff City. The players are, left to right, back row: Nathan Ham (who went on to play for Millwall), Gary Hughes, Mark Phillips, Gareth Roberts, Christian Prygodzicz, Chris Ingram (who went on to play for Cardiff City), Karl Spiller, Craig Davies, Christopher Lewis. Front row: Andrew Davies, Geraint Phillips, Lee Stone, Ross Fitzpatrick, Christian Trott, -?- and holding the cup is Darren Wires.

Known as the Stage Square the road leads to Cwmparc past the Parc and Dare Theatre. It was in the late 1990s that, due to high levels of crime in the area, local businesses gathered together and equipped the streets with CCTV. Many valley high streets are now installing this equipment. The building on the left is the Stage pub and the original post office is opposite, now situated lower down the street. What happened to the Square's lamp nobody knows, many say it ended up on someone's allotment!

Parc and Dare Workmen's Institute was built in 1884 to provide recreational facilities for miners employed by David Davies. The building was paid for by a grant from Mr David with the miners contributing a shilling from their pay. Later in 1913 an extension was built to house a cinema and billiard hall. The Parc and Dare Theatre now seats 690 people and is the venue for local amateur theatre companies as well as the Parc and Dare Theatre Company under the direction of Brian Meadows. This is where all the early plays of Rhondda playwright Frank Vickery were performed.

During 1895 Treorchy Male Voice Choir was known as the Royal Welsh Male Voice Choir of Treorky and its conductor was William Thomas and had only fifty members. One of the founder members of the choir, William Bebb, is pictured in the front row second from the left. The choir sang at many venues throughout the world, one of which was at Windsor Castle in 1895 for Queen Victoria. A recording of the choir is buried under the Empire State building. The choir reformed after the Second World War on 16 October 1946 with Tom Jones and John Haydn Davies appointed as the new music staff. John Haydn Davies was later presented with the MBE by HM Queen Elizabeth II during August 1961.

Their first concert to raise funds for the newly-formed choir was held on 20 July 1947 at Ramah Chapel (see p. 71), collecting a grand total of £12 for their fund. Treorchy was the first male choir to perform in the newly built St David's Hall in The Hayes, Cardiff, on 18 September 1982. Today, the choir has over one hundred members and is conducted by Andrew Badham.

The modern picture shows the choir in November 1999, prior to their month-long tour of Australia. (More information can be found on their web-site: www.treorchychoir.org.uk.)

The home of Dr Armstrong and his brother Fergus (top) was 'Gilnochie House', named after the family ancestral home of the clan Armstrong. Dr Armstrong worked at the Cardiff Royal Infirmary from 1912 having passed his exams at the age of twenty-five at Edinburgh University. Between 1946 and 1951 he performed 500 appendectomies without losing a patient. His work also took him to many parts of the world, meeting many heads-of-state; one such meeting was with Queen Marie of Rumania in Bucharest. While working at Bucharest he was captured and made a prisoner of war in 1916 by the Bulgarians. The enemy wanted to give him a bravery medal but the British Government would not let him wear an enemy decoration in wartime. The Treorchy home was demolished after his retirement and a new library was built and opened on 1 December 1971.

Once a farm, Ystradfechan, was converted into a house by the general manager of the Ocean Coal Company around 1900. It is now used as a home for the elderly.

Ystradfechan House, Treorchy.

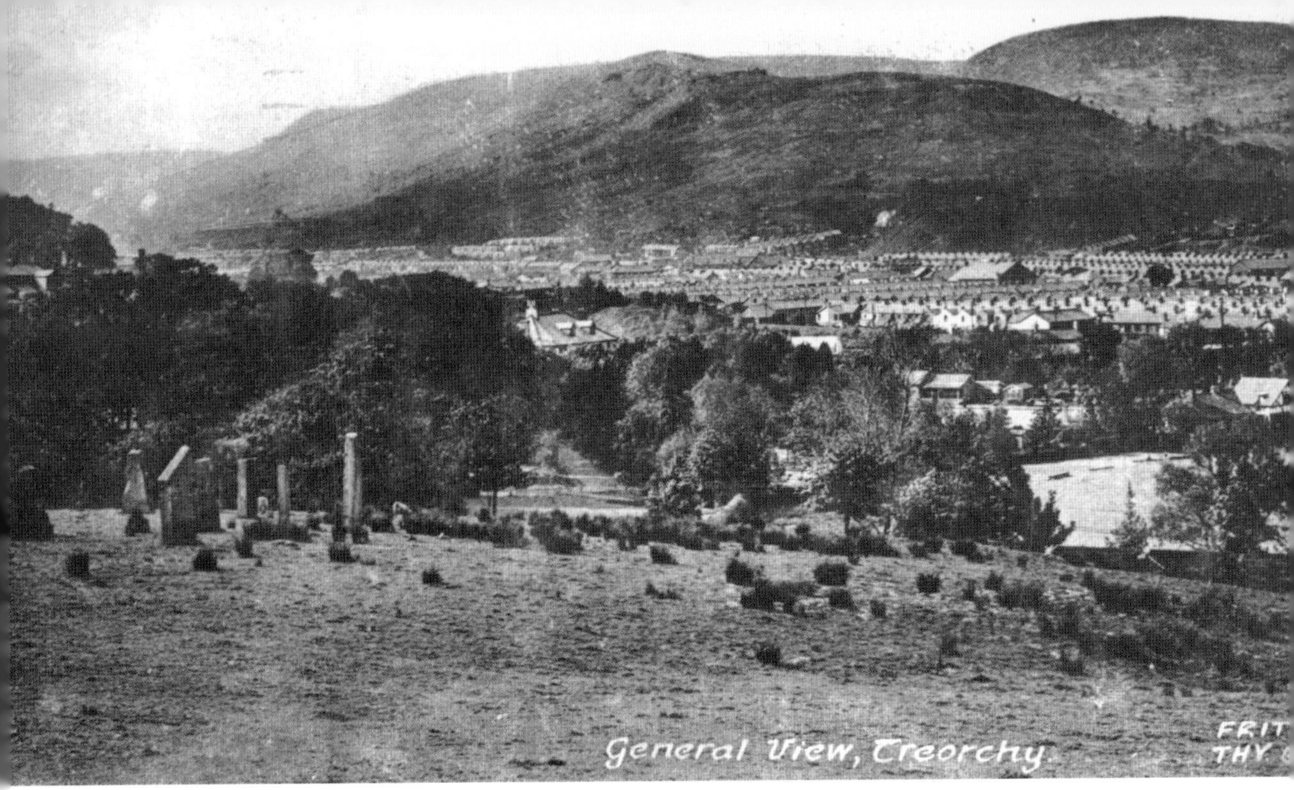
General View, Treorchy.
FRIT
THY

DRUIDS CLOSE

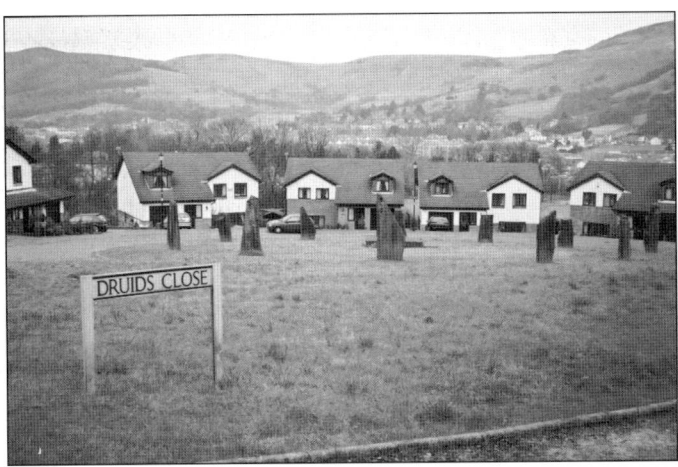

The older picture was taken in 1934 overlooks the Gorsedd Circle where the 1928 Eisteddfod was held. Local roads were widened in preparation for the many Eisteddfod goers. In the early 1990s it was re-developed into a residential area of forty detached homes.

Staff at Pentwyn Cottage Hospital, Treorchy (below), line up for their annual photograph. Built on the site of Pentwyn Farm in 1924 the hospital opened on Thursday 15 January 1925 and was used to treat local colliery accident victims and was funded via subscriptions deducted from local miners' wages, 'every penny in every pound'. From October 1929 until June 1930 the hospital was ordered to close its doors to visitors due to the prevalence of Smallpox sweeping the valley. The hospital finally closed in 1990 and was derelict until 1992, when extensive work was carried out. On 28 June 1993 the premises were re-opened as a privately run nursing home known as 'Ty Pentwyn Nursing and Residential Home' owned by Mr Mukherjee and Dr Chakrabarti of Merthyr (both retired doctors), Mr C. Davies (builder) of Aberdare and Mr C. West (administrator) of Gwent.

A bird's eye view of Pentre taken from St Peters Church tower in 1926 looking towards Treorchy. The colliery is Tynybedw Colliery, sunk in 1876 by Edmund Thomas of Maindy Hall and partner George Griffiths of Pontypridd. Known locally as The Swamp, the mine closed in 1933. Later the area was re-developed by the Forestry Commission who planted trees, ferns and grass. The new picture (right) shows the view in 2000.

High Street, Treorchy

High Street, Treorchy, leading to Pentre showing Tynybedw Colliery in the background and the Red Cow public house on the left. Notice how the street is uneven and how the telegraph poles look as if they're about to fall down!

Chapter 7
CWMPARC
(VALLEY OF PARKLAND)

Construction of Station Road during 1928 at the boundary of Cwmparc and Treorchy. It was in 1898 that Cwmparc and Treorchy became separate parishes from Ystradyfodwg. The first vicar in the new parish was the Revd Thomas Harries. The first street to be built was Railway Terrace in 1886. During the spring of 1963 a sodium lighting system was installed on the main road of Cwmparc and work on the side streets was carried out the following year.

Cwmparc Workmen's Library and Institute Committee on VJ Day 1945. Left to right, back row: D.J. Thomas, Austin Pearce, Idris Thomas, David Thomas. Middle row: Harry Morgan, Charles Holmes, Edward Jones, Trevor Herbert, David Hicks, Glyn Phillips, Griffiths Lewis, Josiah Middleton, Albert Drummon. Front row: J. Chislett, Ed Rees (librarian), Cllr Iori Thomas (life member), H.G. Prosser (secretary), Rufus Roderick (chair), J.H.M. Lewis (finance), Thomas Herbert (life member), Josiah Roderick (billiard marker), Fred Emery. The newly-refurnished hall was rebuilt after a fire.

A group of Cwmparc 'buttes' all aboard for a trip down to the pub (below). Bus trips are still as popular today as they were then. Ladies of Penyrenglyn Carmel Chapel Young Wives group set out for a day at Western-Super-Mare under the direction of supervisor and chair Mrs Mary Evans of Pentre (right). The men below are, left to right, back row: Penry Lewis, Lywsin Bowen, Dick Morgan, Johnny Rees, Donald Davies, Islwyn Bowen, Tom Williams, Fergus Evans. Front row: Bob Peake, Gwyllym Michael and Ben Davies. The women to the right are, left to right: Jean Edwards, Betty Todd-Jones (mother of Pen Pych Headmaster, Gareth), Margaret Williams, Sylvia Hughes, Ceinwen Jones.

General View, Cwmparc.

The Park Colliery (nearest in the picture above) was sunk in 1865 and closed in 1967. Miners wages were distributed in the nearby Tremains Hotel which was used as a pay office; it was later buried under a coal tip and a replacement was built on Parc Road. The Dare Colliery (background) was opened by David Davies in April 1870 and closed in 1964. On its site many years later the local authority built the Alicia Day Centre, named after former borough councillor and Mayor Alice Boxhall.

During the 1920s depression a group of former miners from the Rhondda sang around the United Kingdom on the professional stage calling themselves 'The Six Welsh Miners' (right).

Today, Cwmparc boasts their own Welsh celebrity. Ian Watkins, (pictured wearing a stripy T-shirt), born 8 May 1976. Otherwise known as 'H', he is one of the five singers that make up the pop sensation, STEPS. Before finding fame, Ian, spent many years with local theatre groups such as Spotlight Theatre Company and toured the United Kingdom and Canada with local playwright Frank Vickery in one of his many successful stage plays. Ian joined the band in 1997 and went on to achieve many national and international awards for his music, achieving many UK No.1 singles and with his second album, *Steptacular*, selling over one million copies, achieving 'Platinum' status four times. But unlike many Welsh celebrities, Ian is not afraid to acknowledge his roots and is still as he says 'a Rhondda boy at heart!'

During May 1935 Rhondda residents constructed what they called 'King George Beacons' up-and-down the valley. A similar practice was re-enacted on New Years Eve 1999 to celebrate the dawn of a new millennium. Yet again, beacons were lit up-and-down the highest peaks of the valley. Fire beacons have been used for many celebrations in the area. One of these was in 1910 to celebrate the Coronation of King George and Queen Mary. A large beacon was built on top of Graig-y-Ddelw Mountain in Tynewydd. Weeks of preparation took place by carrying timber and items up the mountain to burn. On the evening of the Coronation it rained, but nevertheless the beacon was lit and was seen for miles around. It was so big that it ignited the peat on which it was built and it burned for days after. Deep trenches had to be dug around it to stop it from spreading down the mountain before it could be put out. Apparently the song 'Keep The Home Fires Burning' meant something different to these beacon constructors.

Through the Years

Pre-1400	People live on the mountain tops overlooking Blaenrhondda on the Rhigos mountain
1400-1500	Land is cleared and crops are planted in the valley. A number of farms and small communities (Penyrenglyn and Ystrad) have been established and a Church is built at Ton Pentre
1536	Wales becomes part of England in the eyes of the law on the request of a Welsh petition to Henry VIII
1547	Edward VI gives land to William Herbert, Earl of Pembroke and Baron of Cardiff
1800	**Population of the Rhondda 542**
1840	Libanus Chapel Treherbert holds its first service on 22 January
1845	On 19 April Mr W.S. Clark, Chief Mining Surveyor to the Marquees of Bute signs an agreement for Lord Bute for the purchase of Cwmsaerbren for £9,000
1851	Bute Merthyr Colliery (steam coal seams) Treherbert is opened. Owned by the Marquees of Bute
1854	Fifty copies of building ground plans for Treherbert Cwmsaerbren are issued on 15 January. Historically, this is the first use of 'Treherbert' noted
1854	The first rows of houses are built. These are Bute Street and Dumfries Street Treherbert and Baglan Street, Penyrenglyn
1854	Ynysfeio Colliery (bituminous seams) Penyrenglyn opens. Owners Thomas, Cope and Lewis
1855	First wagons of coal are transported to Cardiff from Gelligaled now known as Ystrad on 21 December. They were hauled from Cwmsaerbren to Gelligaled by carts
1856	Treherbert Mineral Service commences on the Taff Vale Railway Line on 7 August
1857	The first meetings of Carmel Chapel are held above the Castle Hotel in Bute Street Treherbert
1859	On 20 March Carmel Chapel holds its first service in their newly-built chapel on Baglan Street Penyrenglyn
1867	St Mary the Virgin Church is erected in Treherbert
1867	The Rhondda Valley and Hirwaun Junction Railway is opened
1870	Treherbert police station is opened in Penyrenglyn
1871	Treorchy Cemetery opens
1878	The Rhondda Valley and Hirwaun Junction Railway closes
1879	A lease is granted to build the Tynewydd Hotel
1880	Education becomes compulsory
1883	Blaenrhondda School is built for 153 children and 160 infants
1891	St Albans Church, Tynewydd, is erected on 9 November at a cost of £1,600
1893	The Welsh language is accepted as a class subject in schools
1894	Parc and Dare Workmen's Institute opens
1894	The Rhondda and Swansea Bay Railway Line opened at Blaencwm on 14 December
1895	Treorchy Eisteddfod
1899	*Rhondda Leader* newspaper is first published on 2 December
1901	**Population of the Rhondda is 113,735**
1908	Extension of the tram service from Llwynypia to Treherbert occurred in September
1910	Blaenrhondda to Llyn reservoir tunnel is officially opened
1912	King George V and Queen Mary visit Treherbert on 27 June while on a Rhondda visit
1920	A war memorial is erected in Clyngwyn Road Blaenrhondda
1920	Owing to poor attendance All Saints Church in Penyrenglyn begins conducting their Evening Song in English. Morning service remains Welsh
1921	Treherbert AFC are in the Welsh League
1927	Foundations are laid for Treherbert Cottage Hospital on 19 April
1927	In May the Ynysfeio Railway Bridge Penyrenglyn is officially opened by Councillor Rhys Morgan
1928	Ebenezer Chapel Tynewydd is rebuilt
1936	Treherbert Open-Air Swimming Pool opens
1944	On 5 February Treherbert and district is plunged into darkness for seven hours following the main electric wire installation being damaged by a gale

1944	The Carmel Chapel Augmented Ladies' Choir is formed by Mr Arthur Morgan on 11 March
1947	Blaencwm people form a choral society, later to be known as the Selsig Amateur Operatic Society
1948	Blaenrhondda Carnival with Doreen Beasley being crowned Carnival Queen
1954-1955	Diesel trains replace steam trains on the railways
1963-1964	Fernhill Houses Blaenrhondda are demolished
1967	St Mary the Virgin Church, Treherbert, is demolished
1970	The Gaiety Cinema in Bute Street Treherbert is demolished
1979	Blaencwm is flooded after heavy rain on 27 December
1987	Local gardener Ivor Mace breaks the world record for the Heaviest Kelsae Onion at 8lb 13½oz, winning him an entry into the Guinness Book of Records
1990	First staging of 'Down Memory Lane'. An exhibition of old photographs
1990	D.H. Powell Ladies & Gents Hairdressers, the last shop on Dunraven Street, Treherbert, closed at 1pm on 31 March
1992	On 3 February Carmel Chapel Young Wives, Penyrenglyn celebrate their 300th meeting with a fish supper from Ted's Super Bar
1993	**Population of the Rhondda is 78,504**
1995	Treherbert and District Forum is formed. as a group that improves the local community
1999	Blaencwm, Dunraven and Blaenrhondda Schools are closed
1999	Local chemist and County Councillor Mr Geraint Davies is the first Rhondda Assembly Member to be elected to the National Assembly of Wales on 7 May
1999	On 1 July Powers transfer from Westminster to the National Assembly of Wales
1999	Treherbert Cottage Hospital is demolished on 11 December
1999	St Albans Church Tynewydd is closed
2000	Treherbert and distric Gardening society celebrate their 40th Summer Show

Two Blaencwm pals sit on the moutainside overlooking Blaencwm and reflect on the changes they have seen during their lift